MATTHEW HENSON

Library of Congress Number: 87-32318

Library of Congress Cataloging in Publication Data

Gleiter, Jan, 1947-
    Matthew Henson.

    (Raintree stories)
    Summary: Traces the life of the black explorer who
accompanied Robert E. Peary in his discovery of the
North Pole in 1909.
    1. Henson, Matthew Alexander, 1866-1955—Juvenile
literature.   2. Explorers—United States—Biography—
—Juvenile literature.   3. North Pole—Juvenile literature.
[1. Henson, Matthew Alexander, 1866-1955.   2. Explorers.
3. Afro-Americans—Biography]   I. Thompson, Kathleen.
II. Title.
G635.H4G58   1988   919.8 [B] [92]   87-32318
ISBN 0-8172-2676-1 (lib. bdg.)
ISBN 0-8172-2680-X (softcover)

MATTHEW HENSON

Jan Gleiter and Kathleen Thompson

Illustrated by Francis Balistreri

Raintree Childrens Books
Milwaukee

On the morning of March 1, 1909, Matthew Henson awoke at daybreak. Crawling out of the igloo where he had spent the night, he looked around. On all sides he was surrounded by white. White snow, white ice, white—as far as the eye could see. In a very short time, he would be starting out across that whiteness, bound for a place no one had ever been and no one had ever seen. Between him and his goal, there were four hundred miles of emptiness without a living creature in it.

Matthew Henson was on his way to the North Pole.

In 1909, there were few places left on this earth where no one had ever been. The North Pole was one of those few places. People call it "the roof of the world" because it is the northern-most point on this planet. It is the one place where every other direction, no matter which way you turn, is south. It is not a place as much as it is an idea. The North Pole is in the Arctic Ocean, somewhere on the arctic ice.

Matthew Henson was part of a group of explorers under the command of Robert Peary. Peary had dreamed of beating the ice, of surviving the snow, of "nailing the Stars and Stripes to the Pole," for almost twenty years. The dream had hold of him; it controlled him. He could no sooner forget it than forget to breathe. Henson had tried, with Peary, to get to the Pole twice before. Both times, they had been beaten, beaten by the wind, by the cold, by the great, frozen emptiness. This time they were determined to make it.

The group carried its supplies on sledges—long sleds with wooden runners that were pulled by teams of dogs. The dogs were not pets; they were workers—more wolf than dog, born and raised in the frigid cold of the Arctic. They were vicious fighters and hard to control, but they worked harder and better than any dogs Henson had ever seen before. He had learned to harness and drive them as well as the Eskimos did, and he felt great fondness for the difficult, furry beasts.

Often, when he had finished wrestling the snapping, writhing animals into their harnesses, Henson would pat each of their heads affectionately to show his gratitude.

With Peary and Henson, there were five other
explorers from the United States, twenty
Eskimos, and more than a hundred dogs. As
supplies were used, men would be sent back with
the empty sledges. Only a few men would be left
when the Pole was reached. Matthew Henson
hoped desperately that he would be one of them.

March 1 was the last possible day to leave. Any
later than that, and the group might get to the Pole,
but they would never get back. In the Arctic, six
months of the year are constant darkness and six
months are constant light. The explorers couldn't

cross four hundred miles of ice in the darkness.
But if they waited too long to leave, the summer
sun would melt great stretches of ice before they
could cross it coming back. They would strand
themselves or plunge into the heaving water of the
Arctic Ocean.

So now, at 6:30 in the morning, with early
March's narrow band of light in the sky, the order
came. "Forward! March!" Henson, leading the
group, cracked his whip above his dogs' ears.
"Huk! Huk!" he shouted, and they were off, onto
the frozen sea.

Henson pushed through the snow behind his sledge. It was only when the ice was perfectly smooth that the explorers could steal a few moments' ride. Mostly they pushed while the dogs pulled. When the going was easier, they walked or trotted behind.

On this morning, the ice was rough, so rough that Henson had to chop at hills of ice with an ax to make a way. When the sledge broke, as sledges often did in the rough going, he had to stop to fix it. He couldn't make repairs wearing his thick, fur mittens. But within seconds of taking them off, his fingers froze. He had to thrust them inside his fur jacket and under his other arm to thaw them out. Fixing a sledge was slow, painful work. But he did it as he did all his work, carefully and without complaining. It was not part of Matthew Henson's character to complain.

11

Matthew Henson was an unusual man. He had gone to sea at the age of twelve, an orphan who walked from Washington, D.C., to the Baltimore docks to find a job. Find one he did. During the next six years, he learned sailing, carpentry, and everything else that could be learned on board a ship. At the same time, he read. He read every book he could find and, luckily, there were a lot of books available on that particular ship.

Then, at the age of twenty, he met Robert Peary and signed on as his personal servant for duty in Nicaragua. From then on, Henson went with Peary on every trip of exploration he made—several to the frozen wastes of Greenland and then on unsuccessful attempts to reach the North Pole. He was so skilled and so trustworthy that he quickly became much more than a servant. Intelligent, brave, and used to hardship, he was an explorer himself.

That night when they camped, they had gone twelve miles. The furs they wore all day were their sleeping bags, too. They had long ago discovered that Eskimo igloos were a far better choice than tents that snapped and tore and froze stiff in the wind. Henson had become so good at making igloos that he could build one and be inside it, heating tea over a small stove, in less than an hour.

Breakfast was simple, a dried beef mixture they called "pemmican," a cold biscuit, and tea. Then back to the ice and the back-breaking work of hacking a path. They were no sooner through the worst of that then they came to huge blocks of ice with deep, soft snow between. The dogs sank in the snow to their necks, the men to their knees. And when they were through it, they faced open water.

The ice on the Arctic Ocean does not freeze solidly. The movement of the earth and the pull of the moon's gravity combine to crack the ice and create lanes of water called "leads." Henson didn't know, no one ever knew, how many of these leads would open up between them and their goal.

All he knew was that they had to get across, one way or another. This time, they moved down the lead until they found a place where young ice had formed on the water. As they drove the dogs onto it, they could feel the ice buckle and dip below them. But it held, and then they were across.

The next few days were more of the same. It was so cold that their noses and cheeks turned black with frostbite. They pushed onward, reminded of the need for speed every time they looked at the sky. The band of light grew wider every day. They were racing the sun.

Then on March 5, they were stopped by open water they couldn't cross. This was the "Big Lead." It was a hundred yards across, and the water was black and restless. They had faced the Big Lead before, though they never knew exactly where it would be. And it had defeated them before. There was nothing to do but wait, wait for the lead to freeze over or the great, thick sheets of ice to shift and smash together.

It was hard to wait while the sun sat on the horizon, both beautiful and deadly. Every hour they delayed gave the sun time to creep higher in the sky, gave it more power to strand them.

It was hard to wait while the weather was clear and calm, perfect for traveling. The miles they could have sped across in weather like that!

But there was no choice. For days and days, the south shore of the Big Lead was speckled with dogs and sledges, igloos and men.

Henson saw that his Eskimo friends were
worried and afraid. They were not driven by a
dream to find the Pole. They were just working,
working for the pay of rifles and knives and the
tools that helped them live their lives. Facing the
Big Lead and wondering when it would close was
not work they liked. Wondering if, once it did close,
it would open again before they came back was
work they liked even less.

So one of the other explorers, Donald MacMillan, organized games. There were races, wrestling matches, tugs of war, and weight lifting. It was hard to make the Eskimos understand that they were supposed to try to beat each other. They were a cooperative, not a competitive, people. But the games were fun and broke the spell of dread.

Seven days later, seven days of using up precious food and fuel for the stoves, the Big Lead had frozen over. Across they went, onward again, to the Pole!

Whenever the ice was smooth, they made good time. When they had to ax their way, foot by foot, their progress was slow. Sometimes they crossed hills of ice, tugging and shoving the sledges, men and dogs alike. When they came to leads, they found a way across. Sometimes they looked for new ice and, holding their breaths, raced across. Sometimes they floated across on ice rafts, barely big enough to hold a sledge and its dog team. One slip of a foot or a paw would be the end. But, even when the arctic wind blew in temperatures that dipped to fifty-nine degrees below zero, on they went.

By March 29, there were only three teams left—Peary's, Henson's, and Captain Bartlett's. The others had been sent back. These three teams were stopped by another lead too wide to cross. Grateful this time for a rest, they crawled into their igloos for a few hours of sleep.

Suddenly, sounds like rifle shots woke them. Bolting outside, they saw huge cracks splitting the ice. The ocean was heaving violently, crumbling the igloos and throwing great sheets of broken ice into piles. Henson raced for the terrified dogs. Then, with a roar, a huge crack opened between Peary and Henson's teams and that of Captain Bartlett. Bartlett's team was stranded on a tiny island, a floe of floating ice in the black water, adrift in the pitching sea.

While Peary shouted orders and Henson fought to pull the dogs and sledges to safety on thicker ice, Bartlett's island turned and drifted slowly closer to theirs. The instant the two floes touched, Bartlett yelled and his dogs shot forward, across the narrow crack. Bartlett himself leaped the gap as the crack opened up again.

The group raced for safety on the thick ice. As soon as they reached it, they built new igloos and fell into an exhausted sleep. The next day, the lead froze over and the sledges were driven across ice so thin that Henson could feel it moving under his feet.

On April 1, about 150 miles from the goal, it was time for the last group to be sent back. Bartlett was chosen to return. Commander Robert Peary, Matthew Henson, and four Eskimos—Ootah, Egingwah, Seegloo, and Ooqueah—were ready for the final dash to the Pole. Henson knew they would make it. Make it or die trying.

By April 5, they were one long day's march from the Pole. They came to a lead with floes of floating ice. Partway across, the floe that Henson was balanced on slid from under his feet. He plunged into the water. His thick mittens kept him from grabbing onto the edge of the ice, and the pain of the freezing water crept higher and higher on his body as he sank.

Furious at a fate that would stop him this close to the Pole, Henson struggled in the water, but it was hopeless. Then he felt himself grabbed by the back of his neck. Ootah dragged him up, out of the jaws of death, and across the floe to solid ice.

On April 6, Peary used an instrument called a sextant to determine where they were. They were at the North Pole.

Matthew Henson's reason for living with pain and misery and for facing death was his own deep desire to succeed. And Matthew Henson did succeed. He succeeded at one of the hardest tasks a human being has ever faced.

Luckily for Matthew Henson, he had not hoped for glory or riches or fame. Because Matthew Henson, a black man in a time that seldom recognized black achievement, never got the glory, the riches, or the fame that should have come with his success.